# Godfacts

Also by Dick Williams:

*God Thoughts*
*Prayers for Today's Church* (ed.)

# Godfacts

**Dick Williams**

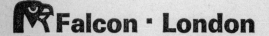
Falcon · London

*First published* 1973
*Copyright* © R. H. L. Williams 1973
ISBN 0 85491 541 9

FALCON BOOKS
are published by the Church Pastoral Aid Society,
Falcon Court, 32 Fleet Street, London EC4Y 1DB

*Overseas agents*
Scripture Union, 177 Manchester Street,
Christchurch, New Zealand

Sunday School Centre Wholesale, PO Box 3020,
Cape Town, South Africa

EMU Book Agencies Ltd, 1 Lee Street, Sydney, NSW,
Australia

Anglican Book Society, 228 Bank Street, Ottawa K2P 1X1,
Canada

*Made and printed in Great Britain by*
*Hunt Barnard Printing Ltd., Aylesbury, Bucks.*

# THE RIGHT TO KNOW

Everywhere I hear
opinions.
Everywhere I encounter
ideas, philosophies, suppositions,
pictures, poems and parables.

Many of them are lovely, some confusing,
But the world is real. The world is a fact.
And I am real. I am a fact.
And whatever caused the world and me to be
is a fact.
And whatever the universe exists for
is a fact.
And whatever the reason for the life I live
that too
is a
fact.
They are facts that I want to know.
They are facts which I feel I have a right to know.

# THE FATEFUL FACT

If there is no reason behind the universe, then
that is a fact, and
it is a fact I need to know.
For if I knew that
I should know that whatever reason I can construct
for living
will be sheer invention
having no authority whatever
save that of my own mind.

But,
if there is a reason for everything
that too is a fact,
and it is even more important that I should know it.

For to be alive for a purpose and to be
ignorant of it
would be a tragedy beyond imagination.

# FIRST FACTS

I begin with the facts of existence, as I am aware of
them :
here we are,
way out in the suburbs of the universe,
biological phenomena characteristic of
a colossal planet which,
when seen as part of all creation is,
microscopically
tiny :
here we are – men on earth.

And there is our sun, that immense
conflagration in the midst of nothingness,
one of the smaller stars, a mere
ninety-one million miles away, and losing weight
at the rate of
two million tons a minute, exporting through space
its heat and light,
some small part of which keeps humanity alive on earth :

There it is
our sun,
and beyond it, the million million other suns
and all the countless presences and promises of
unfathomable
space, deployed through scales of distances and time
which make imagination,
panic, founder and eventually
ignore.

Here we are,
and here am I, a part of it all.

# LOST ENDEAVOUR

I used blithely to hope that somehow my mind would
one day
expand sufficiently
to encompass the whole mystery and majesty of
existence, and enable me to
understand that which is greater even than
existence itself, for
I used to hope
that one day I should be able to understand that which
caused existence
to exist : that for which one word alone suffices –
GOD.

No wonder my mind fell back exhausted,
like a fish trying to fly.
For it was forgetting that it too was simply a part of
what exists :
something which, by definition, is less than, other than
and different from that which
causes
things to exist.

# DAY OF LIGHT

Then came a day of light.
A new thought came, and with its coming
was a hope as bright as day.

I could not think my way to God –
only to the extreme probability of His existence.
But if there were to be a God at all,
then
He would have to be
the maker of my mind,
and, therefore,
greater than my mind.

And from that, two things followed:

One was that I am
constitutionally incapable of
finding Him for myself.

The other was that
He is constitutionally capable of
revealing Himself to me.

The lesser cannot encompass the greater.
But the greater can accommodate itself to the lesser.
And, since that which is greater – GOD –
knows the minds He has created,
the way He might choose to reveal Himself will
be perfect.

# A DIFFERENT SORT OF SEARCH

The thought that this truth might win its way to me
altered the nature of my search,
broadened its base and widened its scope.

I began to look for possible
outcrops
into human experience, and, therefore, into the
history
of anything which might claim to have its origin
elsewhere.

Then came the revolution.

Then what was obvious became visible.
Then what had always been present proclaimed itself.
Then the Jesus of the children's hymns, the Christ
of the Sunday School picture book,
spoke
through the Bible
saying : 'He who has seen me has seen the Father'.

# A NEW KIND OF COMMITMENT

Suddenly the quest for truth was launched
almost frighteningly
upon a final phase. And for the first time,
the heart and will were more reluctant than the mind.
It was the mind, and reason and logic
which said, 'Forward'. It was the heart which hesitated.

For now the search had narrowed down
as through a strait and narrow gate
till it was sharply focused on
one man,
and so became committed to intense investigation of
His life : His words : His deeds. What He was and who
He was.

I could not think Him mad.
I could not think Him bad.
I had to think Him right – completely
right when He said, 'I and the Father are one' . . .
'I am the truth . . . I am life'.

Reason, logic, intellect, all agreed upon the course of
action.
Only the heart paused – paused
as a swimmer about to dive –
then came commitment.

## MORE THAN GENIUS

It was through Jesus I learned that
God speaks and acts and reveals Himself
in many ways.

The Bible is the record of those ways,
in all their variety. That is why
the Bible is such a complicated book.
But that is also why it has such a unity –
GOD
speaking to
man.

And that is why,
when we hear Jesus say:
'He who has seen me, has seen the Father',
we find the entire theme of the Bible is one person:
Jesus.

There is a magnificent simplicity about this.
It is the simplicity of genius –
indeed, of more than genius, it is the simplicity of
GOD.

# DEED INTO CREED

Because God has allowed us to know
what He is like;
because God, the inventor of speech, is Himself
the speaker;
because the source of man's knowledge of God is
God Himself,
the facts of the faith are revealed with supreme
clarity
and complete
authority.

Therefore we state the facts :
we state the facts because they are touchstones of reality;
we state the facts because they are the basis for
co-operative Christian thought;
we state the facts because, so easily, our minds can be
sundered from them, and drift
upon the shoreless seas of speculation.

We state them simply because man is a complicator.
God acted with simplicity in Christ.
But man can take simple things and confound their
purpose
and their meaning. Man
can take a Garden of Eden, a society with no rules
save one,
and produce an urban jungle like our own, choked with
rules and regulations.

And what he does with his life and with society
he does, too, with his thought and faith,
with his philosophy and religion.

# GILDED GALLEON?

Some people I know,
People trying hard to believe in God,
people who sometimes go to church, and even sometimes
sing the hymns,
wince
when it's time to say the Creed.

The Creed, it seems to them, is like a
lordly galleon,
drifting down through the mists of time
upon the deadly reef of modern thought,
heading with lordly trust towards
its intellectual shipwreck.

And they wince because they must either tell a lie and
say
'I believe',
or else they must feel the full weight of this
gilded galleon
grind upon their doubts.

I know the fear, the wincing well;
know it as well as I know the dentist's drill.
For these are friends of mine,
and I, too, have thought like them . . .
. . . before I came to terms with life's central challenge,
that challenge made to intellect as well as heart,
the challenge of the Christ.

# SHAPE OF REALITY

But I have other friends as well, people with
minds as honest as the doubters, and consciences equally
knife edged and strong:
and these friends find the Creed to be
the outward shape of what is real within their minds,
the mould in which their minds have learned to
cast
the molten treasure of God's truth;
a form of words which liberates
their love for God,
a mighty formula to be explored, applied, and loved
for ever.

And nowadays I think like them.
For the Creed sums up what has followed
in man's thinking through the ages
once he has chosen to believe in
Christ.

For if Jesus be the Word of God
the Creed spells out the shape
of reality.

## TOO BIG TO TAME: TOO GREAT TO FLEE

And so we say the Creed,
and here it is again :
so familiar and so strange,
speaking as it does
of mysteries beyond the range of our invention,
but entering, by God's gift, into the mind of man.

And every time I say these words
I cross a continent of truth,
exploring on each journey
the points of endless interest on the way,
and grappling with ideas
too big for me to tame : too great for me to flee.


## THE CREED

I believe in God the Father Almighty, Maker of heaven
and earth :
And in Jesus Christ his only Son our Lord,
Who was conceived by the Holy Ghost, Born of the
Virgin Mary,
Suffered under Pontius Pilate, Was crucified, dead and
buried,
He descended into hell; The third day he rose again
from the dead,
He ascended into heaven, And sitteth on the right hand
of God the Father Almighty; From thence he shall
come to judge the quick and the dead.

I believe in the Holy Ghost; the holy Catholick Church;
The Communion of Saints; The Forgiveness of sins; The
Resurrection of the body, And the life everlasting.
Amen.

# WHO AM I?

I believe!
Who is this 'I'?
And what is it doing when it says: 'I believe'?

Instinctively I know
that to proclaim such a faith as this
is a total act:
a total act of a total personality.

So
before I say 'I believe', I must ask myself some questions.
I must ask
'How well do I know this "I"?'

Perhaps ...
yes, it is dimly possible, so perhaps ...
I do know myself better than anyone else does.
But truly to know oneself is a great achievement.
A nodding acquaintance with literature and
philosophy ...
a smattering of information about great personalities
of history ...
and some of my deeper conversations with my best
friends
combine to assure me that I am not alone in
my estimate of the difficulty.

## CAN DECISIONS DECIDE?

Perhaps I can begin to know myself most truly
in the decisions I make.
For my deepest decisions are those acts
in which what I am
asserts itself
and will not be denied.


## THE DECISION-MAKING COMPONENT

Is there any decision which makes such a comprehensive
and deep
demand upon me that
in making it
'I' declare myself?

I can know many things about myself.
But I can only know myself
in my decisions.

In all the complicated machinery of my personality
it is my true self which is
the decision-making component.

## THE IMPORTANCE OF THE GREATEST DECISION

It is hard to know myself because I did not make myself.
In fact, the whole mystery of life arises out of this
one fact :
that I did not make myself.

If there is a creator it must mean that He is
my creator.
If I can know the one who made me
I can know myself.

And

if knowledge of my creator
depends upon
my choosing to know Him
then
this decision is the greatest decision
I can take.

When I say 'I believe' I am taking that decision.
I believe . . .

# WHAT IS FAITH?

'I believe' means 'I have faith'.
And what is faith?
It is an attitude and an activity, not a commodity –
an activity going on all the time.
It is one of the vital forces of daily life :
it undergirds and stimulates all thought and action;
it is an essential part of all that makes us
human.

We have many powers. Prominent among them are
the powers to wonder, question, test, explore, experiment
and decide.
And underlying all these powers is faith :
the faith
that the exercise of all these powers is
worthwhile.

Faith – this sort of faith – is a native function
of the mind.
Faith – this sort of faith – is so much a part of life
that we are apt to forget that it is there at all.
Faith – this sort of faith – is the principal plank
of rational thought.

This sort of faith is generous in its ways.
It even sponsors doubt – the sort of doubt which lives
to find out what is false and what is true.

# WHAT IS DOUBT?

When I say 'I believe' I do not, therefore, say
'I have no doubts'.
For doubts are the tools of faith,
and faith can wield them well.

The men who build an aeroplane, or rockets to the
moon,
are acting upon their faith.
But
these same men will systematically doubt
every nut, bolt and wire,
every concept, calculation, structure and device
involved in what their faith creates.
For them
faith without doubt would be lethal.

But very clearly, for them,
doubt is so much less than faith.
It is faith which is the context and the home of doubt,
– it is not the other way round.
And this they declare in deed and action, for
when all their doubts have had their exercise
and when all that separates faith from knowledge is
trial, experiment, venture
then . . .
then they act upon their faith.

And so men fly, and so they travel to the moon . . .
and beyond.
For man needs more than his mind to find out truth.

# INVENTOR OF REASON

I am a child of my age
therefore,
so far as religion (if not anything else) is concerned
I have been brought up to respect the role
which reason has to play.
In fact I have been brought up to venerate reason –

It was on the tip of my tongue to say
'worship'
reason. But that would not have been exactly true.
For my early influences were not towards
idolatry –
not even such sophisticated idolatry as that which
replaces truth
with the apparatus by which we sometimes find it.

Reason is a tool, an implement.
Man must not worship reason, no matter how brightly
it shines
but certainly
he must venerate it. For faith in God is
faith in the inventor of reason.

# REASON AND REVELATION

In all their generations it seems that men
have discovered truth in two different
(though related)
ways.

Like men who build aeroplanes and spaceships,
they have reasoned their way towards conclusions
in which they have subsequently placed their faith
by risking their lives.

And they have also
found truth break in upon them
from outside the circle of their enquiry
like men who meet Jesus.

In becoming a Christian
I discover truth in both these ways.

# FAITH ISN'T FEELING

Faith is not a feeling.
And my decision to believe in Christ
does not depend upon my feelings, for my faith
is not the expression of my emotional response
to the interaction in my mind of
nature, society, Bible and Church.

My faith is the expression of my choice.
It is in every respect, except that of its content,
similar to the faith of the atheist – the man
who says 'I believe there is no God'.
It is like the faith of the agnostic who says
'I believe that reality is so constituted that
we can never know whether there is a God or not'.

For whatever our faith
it is something we have chosen
upon the basis of reason
in the face of available evidence.

I say 'I believe in God' because
my reason,
in the face of the widest range of evidence I can observe,
can reach no other conclusion than this :
that God is
and that we have seen Him in Christ.*

*I have given my reasons for these conclusions in my
book *Godthoughts*.

# FROM ONE EXTREME TO THE OTHER

But feelings are important to me still.
Sometimes they reinforce my choice,
sometimes they question it.

Sometimes, Lord, there are mornings when
I awake to stark unbelief.
I find it present with me
in me
part of me . . .
more,
I find it to be myself :

I myself am unbelief.

And sometimes, Lord, I half wake in the night
and know Your presence.
Sometimes there is a sense almost of an
embrace,
not quite a lover's embrace,
but a maker's embrace,
or perhaps that firm grip of what,
for all I know,
may be an angel.

This is not a matter of faith, it is a matter of knowledge.
And so my feelings can swing between these two poles.

# GETTING IT RIGHT

I thank You, Lord, for my feelings:
for their range and variety
and their capacity to impress upon me
the sign'ficance of life
and of its happenings.

I thank You that they can support
courses of action which are right.
I thank You too, that they can weaken and contest
projects and philosophies which are wrong.

Help me to take note of my feelings, Lord,
and to understand them:
but may I not be ruled by *them*.

May the basis of my action be rational.
May my decisions be informed by knowledge,
shaped by understanding,
defined by judgement, and brought to birth by
wisdom.

## THE FACTS BEHIND THE FEELINGS

I must not forget that
feelings of faith and feelings of unbelief
are, quite simply, feelings. That is to say,
they are what I generate for myself, and
I am their author.
And I have noticed certain things about them.
For instance
as long as I am thinking about those things in life which
change – knowledge, for example, or
political systems, or applied sciences . . .
advances in medical research, space travel, and any form
of technology, or the fashions
of literature, art or society :
as long as my mind is absorbed in these things,
(and I don't mean 'aware' of them, but I do mean
'absorbed' in them), then for so long my feeling of faith
in Jesus Christ is apt to go into decline, until, suddenly
in turning to think of Him again,
my mind encounters what seems suddenly unreal.

But
when I am thinking about those things in life which do
not change . . .
our mortality for instance, our sin, our appetites for
good things
or for bad, our desires for goodness, beauty, truth : the
need for true relationships with other people and with
society;
the continual threat of disease, even in a healthy body,
and the certainty of death :
the impermanence of all the things among which we
move,

the conundrum of creation : the facts behind the
phenomena, and
all the possible answers to the question 'Why?'
*then* my feeling of faith grows stronger, for then
I relate my life to those things
to which Christ related His own life, and
then
my lifelong choice of faith finds reinforcement from my
feelings.

Of course I must always be interested in
those things which change. But I must not mistake them
for the whole of life.
To ponder them alone is to be cut off from life itself :
the great continuum which abides.

For a mind which feeds on things that change
can leave behind the real world
in a supposed quest for
reality.

A true realist must always tackle the things which do
not change.
It is only from a constant dialogue with these, that he
can understand the things which do.

## THE TRUTH AND I

I believe.

Belief is an activity of mind and spirit,
the activity sparked off by an encounter
with truth.

Belief is not some thing I possess,
it is not a chattel, it is not an attribute of my character,
it is something which
I do.

It is an activity which I engage in when I encounter
truth.

## GOD

I believe in God.
What is 'God'?
Many definitions are abroad, but none of them
detain me for a minute
except one : 'God is
the creator of the whole universe'.
That is the only idea of God which has the power to
detain me,
but that is the idea which detains me
perpetually.

If there is no creator there is no God.
But, if there is a creator, then
I am concerned to know Him.

God.
A little word. A tiny word.
Just one trim and solid syllable
which can be uttered in a fraction of a second.
But a word which can stand for more than
all the vocabularies of
all the languages
of all the world in all its ages.

God is the most useful
of words,
but it is also the most
misused
and can be the most empty.

It all depends on the way in which I use it,
the spirit in which I use it,
and what I do with my life –
with my heart, and mind and body,
as I use it.

Let me use that word well now, as I say
I believe in God.

# I'VE NEVER STOOD ON EVEREST

I've never stood on Everest
and I don't suppose I ever will
but,
when people talk about Hillary and Tenzing and
those rare men who like them, scale the incredible
heights
I have a very clear sense of what they see and feel.
Mention Everest to me, and my mind
immediately inhabits
an area of mental geography which is quite real.

However,
I have no doubt
that if by some incredible chance
I should ever reach the place which imagination
flies to in a moment,
and stand upon that peak above the clouds
thrust on dazzling whiteness into a sky that's cloudless
black,
the reality would be immensely different
from what I imagine with such confidence now:

why then do we picture to ourselves such places at all?

It would be then just as on that day when, setting foot
in Canada, my old 'adventure-book-geography lesson'
pictures of that land were swallowed up in exciting new
reality.

But yet, if it had never been for those old 'pictures'
I should never have got there at all. Indeed
those old pictures were not destroyed by the reality:
they were fulfilled, rearranged, integrated, enlarged and
then subsumed.

And so I don't abandon my mental pictures of unvisited
places . . .
Moscow, Samarkand, Peking and Nepal. To do so would
be to change the very nature and instinct
of the mind. It would be to
limit, restrict, curtail the range of my sympathies for,
interest in, involvement with
the rest of the world. It would be
to act at a sub-human level.

Lord God, I have never seen *You*. How then
shall I regard the picture which finds its shape
around Your name
within my mind?

As totally without value?
Or like my 'view from Everest'?
Like my childhood thoughts of Canada before we went
to live there?
That is to say, like a guide which was less than the
reality, but a true guide just the same.
Impressions formed from pictures, books and hearsay
can be firmly related to the reality they depict
provided they are held with humility. And
what is true for geography is true, I think, of
theology, too.

# MY PICTURE OF GOD

What is my picture of God, now?

It is of Jesus
transposed into eternal perspectives and cosmic
dimensions and unlimited power.
Despite the essential truth of this,
I have no doubt that it falls immensely short
of that reality which is.

But when I see You, Lord,
I believe that my growing image of God will declare
itself as one which has been a true guide.

Jesus said, 'He who has seen me, has seen the Father',
and He gives us the Spirit of sonship which grows in
the knowledge of the Father.

'Father'.
I have to face the fact that this word
reaches inside my defences and belongs there.
I have to face the fact that my idea of fatherhood
necessarily
took its first form and shape and substance
from the man who was my father : a dear, beloved man.

The idea of fatherhood
was the imprint upon my mind and soul
of that benevolent giant of my infancy.

It became a notion which united two elements which
sometimes we separate :
the element, first of intimate affection,
an affection which was a presence entirely within the
circle of my defences, perfectly at one
with what I was.
And then too, there was the element of authority :
that other presence, one that was
set over against me, whose bidding – sooner or later –
I did.

Yet both were linked, for both were one. And along the
link, along the axis between the presence which was
over against me, and the presence which was within me
– between authority and love –
communication flowed.
Neither he, nor I, were perfect, but the relationship
worked and so the notion of fatherhood took shape.

# A NEW VIEW OF THE SAME THING

Time has gone on.

'Father' is a word which has grown as
experience itself has grown. No longer is it limited
to the impression made upon a child by his own father,
now it is a word which denotes present experience,
an experience which is bracketing together
the middle years of this particular life.

Now fatherhood means a constant counterpoint
of joy and sorrow, hope and fear, success and failure,
power and impotence, peace and pain :
all the nerve ends of life
are exposed to the relationships of parent to child.

This too helps me to think about
what Jesus meant when He spoke to God as Father
and encouraged us to do the same.

'When you pray' said Jesus, 'say "Our Father" '.
And that is Good News almost beyond believing.

# SOMETHING OF YOU

O God, our own experience of parenthood,
as fathers or mothers, and
our experience of parenthood as
sons or daughters,
alike and reveal to us something of Your immense
involvement in creation : something of Your
concern for Your children.

How complete Your knowledge, how vast Your love,
how immense Your interest, how profound Your
involvement :
how far beyond the nerveless fingers of our imagination
lies Your capacity to
love, create, uphold, suffer, rule, judge, forgive, make
perfect.

# BEYOND THE FRINGE

But my mind is still only on the fringe of
what can be meant by 'Fatherhood',
for God was Father before the first man begat the
first son.
It is because God is Father that we exist.
And while our notion of His Fatherhood is bound up
in so many ways
with our experience as children
and with our experience as parents,
there is one influence greater and more powerful
even than these.
And we feel the force of it in Christ.

For Jesus called God 'Father'.

And He said :
'Nobody knows the Father but the Son and
him to whom the Son will reveal Him'.

# CHRIST'S VIEW OF THE FATHER

Is it possible for me to get inside the mind of Jesus
and see what He meant when He said 'Father'?

In part it may be. And I shall try. And though I know
it will take more more than a lifetime to succeed, and
that success will only come eventually
as a gift
I will make the attempt.

Jesus said : 'I do what I see the Father doing'.
He said : 'My Father works, and I work'.

In the experience of Jesus, it seems quite clear,
the Fatherhood of God
was not something
static.

It was the heavenly side of a relationship
which was totally dynamic : and He understood
His own life and activities in terms of their
correspondence to
the character and action of the One he called Father.
He knew the Father as a person. And He knew Him as
an active, busy, creative person.

*********

The Father and His work were
an inspiration and guide
to the man who was His Son.
And in His praying, Jesus would observe
His Father's activity, seeing
what He was about, and taking
this to be
the pattern for His own activity,
the programme for His own life.

*********

Jesus also said:
'I am revealing in words what I saw
in my Father's presence'.
When Jesus looked at the world
He was sharing a viewpoint held also by the Father.
He not only looked to the Father, He looked
with
the Father. They looked at life together.
And there is here a deeply delightful
revelation
of their partnership.
It seems that in the relationship of Jesus with His Father,
'Fatherhood' and 'Partnership' were not
mutually exclusive terms.

*********

But He also said:

'I have been taught of my Father'.
His words and His deeds were the outward expression
in Jesus' life
of His relationship with the Father.
In this closest of close relationships – one
possible only with God –
Jesus was our pioneer.

And one night He said, 'Not my will but thine be done'.
And the Father led Him through the shadows where
He cried, 'My God, my God! Why hast thou forsaken
me?'

Then came the words:
'Father, into my hands I commend my spirit'.

And it was the Father
who raised Him;
and it was the Father who exalted Him.

# GOD, THE FATHER ALMIGHTY

O God
we call You Father before we call You
Almighty.
We call you Father before we call you
Maker.

Jesus called You Father. He taught His disciples
and He teaches us
to call You Father, too.

The fact that You are Father is the most
distinctive thing
about the way Jesus spoke *to* You, and spoke *of* You.

And in the Creed we call You Father
before we call You 'Almighty', and before we call
You 'Maker'.
For the word 'Father' discloses Your character,
disposition, attitude, motive.

The word 'Maker' tells us what You do.
The word 'Almighty' tells us about the resources which
are within Yourself.
But the word 'Father' sums up what You *are*.
And because it tells us what You are
it tells us how You employ Your power.
For it is as Father that You
create.
And it is as Father that You are
Almighty.

# MAKER OF HEAVEN AND EARTH

But
some people say
that there was no creation
and that the whole universe is from everlasting to
everlasting,
without beginning, without end.

In that case
there can be no power greater than the powers of
the natural universe,
and so – it follows – there can be no
creator,
and so – it follows – there can be no
God.

Some people say that there was a beginning, but that
it was an accidental one; that there was
some causeless, cosmic accident which set in motion
the whole process of creation.

But
accidents do not happen in a void.
As a minimum requirement
accidents need
conditions
in which it is possible for them to occur.

I cannot conceive of true nothingness
in which anything remotely like an
accident
could possibly occur.

So I must have done with the idea of an
accidental beginning to the universe or else
accept some sort of a creator —
a creator of
(at very least)
those *conditions* in which an accident may occur.

The debate really must be
between those who say there was no beginning at all
and those who say there was.

Those who say there was no beginning
are bound to say
that matter is eternal and for ever.
Those who say that there was a beginning
are bound to say
that between nothingness and the beginning
stands some thing more than an accident :
that between nothingness and the beginning
stands
the Beginner.

# ALL THINGS OF NOTHING

Unless one is to believe that matter is eternal and for
ever and, therefore, that there cannot be a creator,
and that, therefore, there cannot be a God –
one must believe that there was a beginning.
And if one is to believe in a beginning
it follows that one must believe
that before the beginning there was
nothing.

Imagine that!
But no, that's something which I can't imagine.
No one *can* imagine nothing.
True 'nothingness' is beyond our comprehension.

'In the beginning was the Word . . .
. . . and the Word was with God . . . and
the Word was God'.

That is very different from saying that in the beginning
there was nothing. Yet
God – if there is a God – must have made
all things of nothing. No other idea of God is possible.

In the beginning – so far from there being
nothing
there was God.
The unimaginable – God,
together with
the inconceivable – nothing.
Two equal mysteries, but
the one greater than the other, for
with God there was initiative, and power, and mind,
and purpose and achievement.

And that which we cannot imagine – nothingness –
in the presence of God
ceased to be.
God said, 'Let there be light'. God said, 'Let us make'.
God said, 'It is good'.

And I believe in God.


## FIRST WORD

'In the beginning,' said St John,
'was the Word. All things were made by Him'.
All things . . .
and I cannot begin to guess what
'all things'
are.

I cannot imagine the universe.
It is so vast, so diverse, so complex as to be
beyond the range of human imagination.
And every tick of the clock adds to the sum total of its
colossal history and –
as if by a geometric progression –
puts the dimension of the problem
further light years
beyond the range of my mind.

But 'all things' were made by this Word,
and this 'Word' – so runs the heart-stopping claim –
became flesh, and dwelt among us,
and we beheld His glory :
this 'Word' was, and is, Jesus.

# CONCEPT INTO CREATION

He, so it is said, is the Word
by which the worlds were made.
How can I begin to cope with such a thought?

If an architect is to design some great new building
he will need to have the
germ
of an idea
at the very beginning.
The idea must be capable of growing into a concept.
The concept must be capable of statement :
it must have purpose, function and form.
And having these things, it must be capable of
translation into fact.

# THE UNIVERSE WITHIN OUR GRASP

So
somewhere at the foundation of things, in the heart
of things,
in the potential and the pattern of things,
in the origin, destination and present course of things
is a purpose, a power and a process
emanating through one foundation
pattern : the Word of God.

God is the originator. He is life itself and creator of life :
but the whole concept of creation,
the pattern and the purpose of His creative act,
is to be found in Christ Jesus.

And
Jesus can be known.

*This* puts the universe within our grasp.

# FEAR OF THE FUTURE?

Who knows what lies hidden in the Word of God?
As a flower is hidden in a seed,
the future of the world is hidden in the
Word of God.

Ignorance of the future need bring no fear,
for what lies hidden in the Word
is hidden in Christ,
the Word by which the worlds were made.

Who knows what is enmeshed into the processes
of the present, or
what is coming to birth in the travail of today?

We shall not fear
for He who set in motion the process
is its companion, its fellow wayfarer and its Lord.

We shall welcome the future for it brings Him.

# MAKER

There's something inside man which makes him a maker.
Put man in a landscape
and the landscape starts to change.
Let man start to breathe
and things begin to happen.
For man is a maker. His instinct to make
is rooted into his very nature.
For
God made man in His own image.
And man's power to make is the mark of his maker
upon him.

Jesus Himself – completely the Son of God –
said, 'I do what I see the Father doing'.

God is a maker – *the* Maker.
Lord, we love You for that. We cannot doubt that
Jesus would have felt His sonship in a special way
in the carpenter's shop,
making things.

That is why we are set free –
liberated and fulfilled –
when we are making things.

# HEAVEN AND EARTH

Maker of heaven.
Maker of the immaterial.
Maker of that which cannot be weighed, measured,
computed.
Maker of that which cannot be seen.
Maker of those things which some men say
do not exist.
Maker of heaven and maker of earth.
Maker of matter,
and of all material things.
Knowing the innermost structure, the deepest secret,
of everything that can be
weighed, measured, computed :
deviser of everything which men can contemplate,
all that he can touch, and count upon as sure and
certain facts.

Maker of earth – maker of the brain.
Maker of heaven – maker of what the brain can conceive
but the hand cannot touch.
Maker of heaven and earth.

## MAKER OF 'EVOLUTION'

The voice that said 'Let there be light!'
The hand that took red earth between Tigris and
Euphrates and moulded a man;
the breath that struck into clay and gave life.
All minds can see in this the one clear message
that God is creator.
So what of evolution?
Whatever the fact at the heart of the theory
it too is a child of God, the work of His own hands.
The slow harvest of immemorial aeons
bearing fruit
in rock, and soil, and fruit and animal —
eventually too in man —
this is the product of a process with a pattern :
and that pattern is the Word of God
by which all things are made.
God provides the pattern : God begins the process :
God sustains it to its end.
Evolution is a syllable
in the Word of God.

## MAKER OF MEN

God, you gave Your children
freedom.
When You made man
You made him in love, and for love,
and then You gave him
his freedom.

Adam, we are told, could do as he pleased, apart from
one solitary prohibition; and he was given the power
to disregard that too
if he chose.

And so the Bible says in great and ringing tones, that
the origin of manhood is
goodness with liberty :
God's goodness and man's liberty.

It follows, therefore, that life as we know it –
all of history, and all of our own experience – is
what evolves from that 'goodness with liberty'.

# MAN'S CONTRIBUTION

But
'goodness' and 'liberty'
do not sum up the whole of my experience of life,
nor of the life of the world.
In all his generations, man has abused his freedom.
Created for love, he hates.
Created for truth, he lies.
Created for life, he kills and he dies.
Made for heaven, he conceives, constructs, and
embellishes his hell.

'By man came death'.
Man has contributed many things to the tiny part
of the universe he inhabits – things good and bad –
But this is his distinctive
contribution.
'By man
came death'.

O Lord, I confess the sinfulness of what I am;
and my share of the blame.
So how can any of us thank You enough for the
Resurrection of Jesus?
For man's role in creation has been transformed
because
'by man came also the resurrection of the dead' – and
in the midst of death we are in life.

# MAKER OF MY MIND

The maker of my mind . . .
how can I picture You? I cannot,
for I cannot even comprehend the greatness of creation.
I try to imagine the universe and
imagination founders in the attempt,
falls spread-eagled and dies amid the dust of its own
designs.
So how can I imagine that which is greater
than creation?

How can I imagine You, God?
Am I even right to try?
For to fashion in my mind an image of Yourself
might lead me to worship that image . . .
and that is idolatry:
to worship the work of my own mind
as pagans worship the work of their own hands.

Any picture which my mind could paint of You, O Lord,
is bound to deny Your deity, and become
an idol for myself to worship and for others
to deride.

That is why Jesus brings good news.
That is why I turn again and again with ever greater
hope to Him.
For here was one who said,
'He who has seen me has seen the Father'.

And what the mind cannot conjecture for itself,
the Father can disclose.
And the mind which cannot manufacture the image of
its maker, triumphantly may become His mirror.

# OUT OF THE STAINED-GLASS WINDOW

I only awake to God when I measure myself against
one
who is most completely alive, so fully alive as to
be able to
live for others, and
to die for others :
Jesus, the man for others.

There was a time when He was comfortably contained
within the pages of the Bible, locked away
in stained glass windows, moulded
in marble,
petrified upon a plinth.

Then came the day when I looked beyond the narrative
to the event,
looked beyond the portrait to the original,
and put myself in the same room as the reality.

There is so much about myself that I cannot and do
not know,
'Who am I?' I cannot really say, except that
when such a one as Jesus says
'Follow me',
I have found that, riddled with error as I am,
what is at the core of me must say
'Yes'.

# NEW CONTENT FOR 'GOD'

Simply to believe in a 'god'
is not the same as
to know
God.

And truth breaks in upon
faith,
when we meet Jesus.

Jesus puts new content into the word 'god'.
What follows faith in Christ
affects the view we take of all that is,
our view of all being, past, present and future —
everything beyond our ken and within it,
all comes within the sphere of this new influence.

The effects upon belief which flow from faith in Christ
find form for their substance
in the Creed.

# 'WHOM DO MEN SAY THAT I AM?'

I thank You, Lord, that as the years go by
I see You more clearly.

And I thank You that it is through the ups and downs
of life
that You help me to see more deeply into the fact
of Your friendship.

For
all the joys and sorrows, encounters and adventures,
times of desolate prayer and happy fellowship,
exalted worship, and serious slogging work,
all pains, all pleasures,
cross-referenced
by prayer
through Christ
impress upon me, in growing definition, the awareness of
that personality which is
You.

As I follow in the way, Lord, I begin to
know You.
Having known You all these years by faith
I find the fringes where faith and knowledge
interchange and I begin to
know.

# THE KNOWLEDGE OF GOD, IN CHRIST

Lord Christ,
when You were on earth,
how did you think about Yourself, and the Father,
and the Spirit?
What went on in Your mind?

The only way I can begin to try and find answers
to these questions
is by imagining myself into Your place, into
a sense of Your particular calling, into
the attitude to God the Father revealed in Your
prayers to Him,
into Your attitude to creation
revealed in Your miracles and resurrection.

But the central mystery is
impenetrable. And the Bible tells us so.
'No one knows the Son but the Father'.
So it is written.

I partly accept and partly rebel against
the impossibility of knowing.
For
as a human being
there must be so much of the human being Jesus, that
I can understand.

On the other hand, however,
as a sinner,
there must be so much of the Son of God –
even of His humanity – that I
cannot understand.
And as a creature, how can I understand the mind
of one completely united with the creator?
'No one knows the Son but the Father'.

Why, I cannot even understand my deepest friends
in the way they understand themselves,
not really!
How much greater the mystery in the case of Christ.
And yet, and yet . . .
Jesus is the Word by which the worlds were made, and
the Word became flesh.
And what is wonderfully true is that
this Word comes to dwell in all those who
receive Him. He comes to be more fundamentally
a part of us
than our own ego.

And where imagination and theology must always fail,
worship, adoration and communion
unlock the inner recesses of our humanity
and there we begin to know
Him.

For 'no one knows the Father but the Son, and him
to whom
the Son will reveal Him'.

Jesus, You make known to us the one who knows You.

# THE RELUCTANT BIBLE READER

Lord, I thank You for the Bible
and for the way in which, through its pages,
You reveal to men
things which they could never work out for themselves.
I am sorry that I do not know it better, and
I am sorry that, knowing it as well as I do,
I do not read it more.
But
in spite of myself,
in spite of my wandering thoughts, my distractions –
my consent to distraction –
in spite of my wish to have this Bible reading
over
so that it can be considered done and – with it –
my duty; in spite, above all, of my
evasion of prayer as the best and truest
consequence of reading what I've read today –
in spite of all this, in spite of *myself;*
I have seen more of the truth this morning.

Forgive me, Lord, and help me not to run away from
the growing edge of experience
touched to painful exhilaration by the Bible
today.

For it isn't that I shrink from what You are showing me,
it is simply that what I begin to see is
so big, that I know that to grapple with it,
will require much more time and labour than
I want to give just now.

But Lord, the time is here, really.
Help me now to think about it, and grant that
what I am not able to do for myself,
what my mind is not large enough, nor supple enough,
nor
skilful enough to comprehend,
You will disclose to me.

Above all, Lord, grant that
what I have glimpsed
agonizingly, tantalizingly,
today,
may be mine as a seed which may not be snatched away.

# ME AND HIM

'Jesus drew near and went with them . . .'

I can go about my business day by day,
go on and on through life in fact,
with my attention,
my imagination, fear, hope, desire,
centred
upon myself :
the walls of my own mind being the boundary of
my interest,
the pains and pleasures of my body being the arena
of my sensitivity,
myself my one companion.

Some people think of this as the sort of independence
which leads to maturity.
But I know it to be self-regard,
and slavery.

For I *can* go about my business, differently, and
I *can* go on through life in another way.
My companion can be Christ.
My consciousness can be woven around Him :
He can be the centre of my affection;
He can be the focus of my life.
The boundary of my interest can be His, and
He can be the sphere of my sensitivity.

Some people think that this is the posture of a
dependent spirit
the mark of a spiritual cripple
the mentality of the immature.

They could, of course, be right
if I were other than myself and if
Christ were other than He is.

To rely upon myself, is to use my picture of myself
as a cripple uses a crutch. And once
I think ill of myself, my crutch collapses.
So therefore, I must cheat myself and lie
and never know myself for what I am,
if I am to think of standing upright in this world.

To rely upon Christ
is to rely upon one who commands me to be whole,
who bids me think of others, who requires that
I give Him the right
to make on me the ultimate demands of life.
My failures then do not become the ultimate fact of life
for no matter how great these may be,
the ultimate and greatest fact in my life is
Christ's claim upon me, His love for me, His purpose for
me
abiding and eternal, and His forgiveness.

This is perfect freedom. This is the way to true
humanity.

# THE REAL TREASURE

'As you have received the Lord Jesus,
so walk in Him . . .'

When I received You, Lord, with the full powers and
consent of mind and will; when I laid my life on the
line,
when the forces which were within me came together,
when by coming to Christ I came to myself :
then the centre of my life was one with Him who is
the centre of creation.

How I need to get back to that simplicity of heart.
To make progress I must regress,
I must grow by becoming smaller
I must gain ground by losing it.
I must lose my life
to find it.

For I want Christ in my heart,
Him
not just my idea of Him,
not just my image of Him,
not just my rationalization of Him.
not just the thought of Him
either,
in sacramental terms, or
theological terms, or
metaphysical terms, but
Him
as He eternally is
reigning, ruling, directing, forgiving – and alive.

# BROTHER JESUS

O Jesus,
companion,
elder brother,
light which lightens everyone born into the world :
light present at my birth, You
have been with me all my days.

O Jesus, Saviour,
You spoke and one day made me listen :
You called and one day made me follow;
You knocked and one day found my heart's door open.
You have been within me since that day.

O Jesus, king and master :
You come to me in this moment,
You take from my heart the weight of disobedience,
You command
and give me freedom
in obeying.

O Jesus, Word of life,
I fall at Your feet as one that is dead
and in my extinction
I hear You say :
'Rise up! Live! Go!'

# CONCEIVED BY THE HOLY GHOST

O Holy Spirit of God
the minds made for Your habitation
no longer know how to think about You.
Teach us. For You are
the life of God Himself, concerned with all creation
and concerned, too, with us as part of it.

You make possible our relationship to the universe,
and You make possible
our relationship to the Father, through Jesus Christ
the Son.

Holy Spirit, present at creation, source of all matter,
mightier
than all matter,
all man's new beginnings are in You.

Creator Spirit, source of life, and fountain head of
flesh and blood,
we rejoice to know that
in the womb of a strong and humble girl,
You were the source of that life
known to history and to us,
as Jesus.

# BORN OF THE VIRGIN MARY

Remote in time that birth,
distant and dwindling in the perspective of age.
Sometimes I feel it happened much too long ago :
that ancient history cannot be important for
today.

Then I remember a day more ancient still.
A day so deeply buried in the mists of time
there could not be a date to mark the spot ...
the day when someone made a
wheel
and in so doing,
changed the world.

Is that day too ancient to have meaning now?
How could it be? Now, when the whole world runs
on wheels.
The thought which found its triumph in a wheel
is contemporary with each present day.
While men have limbs, no time will come
when that forgotten day will lose its power.

Is it not so with Christmas?
Is it not so with the whole of that human life
of Christ?
Is it not so with His death?
Is it not so with His resurrection?
Those ancient days are always part of today.
Nothing can be more contemporary than they !

# WHEN CHRIST WAS BORN

When Christ was born
the peoples of the world were few : for
He was born close to the roots of human growth.
Perhaps it is not so much a question of His being
born too long ago, but
of His being born
soon enough.
For when the family of man was small,
the peoples who believed in Him
could bear within their growth the influence of His life
and so,
among the surging millions of the world –
multiplying in every generation till
the globe is thronged –
the impulse of His love and truth is found.

The world is sick for lack of Him.
But if He had not been born
at such a time,
perhaps the human race may not have grown at all.
The world is sick for lack of Him. And if He had
not come at such a time,
how much less could history have digested
the prodigious fact
that God
was in Christ.

# WHAT GOD'S LOOKING FOR

Thank You, Lord, for calling someone
like Mary
to be the mother of Jesus Christ our Lord.
There is something infinitely encouraging
in the knowledge that she was
a girl of humble stock :
betrothed to a carpenter; and cousin to the wife
of a priest.

You did not seek her for her social graces,
nor for her intellectual power –
though for all I know, she may have been well blessed
with all – but what You sought in her was
the spirit
of one who, for love of You, would dare all things
and set at risk her
marriage, home, respectability, and the future itself.

'Be it unto me even as thou wilt', she said.
And in the saying of it, showed
the spirit of one fit to make a home for Your own Son;
the spirit of one who would understand the spirit
of her son.

What you sought and found in Mary, Lord,
You seek in us, today. A heart to say 'Your will be done'.
May You find what You are looking for, O God,
in Your church, and in me.

# THE HIDDEN YEARS

In its chronicle of Christ events,
the Creed leaps
from His birth to His death.
It makes no mention of the course and content of
that marvellous life
which links the two.

And there is power in the omission.
For the meaning of the life is in the death.
And Calvary is like a mirror
reflecting
at the far end of a long and glorious pathway
the aggregated images of the way:
resolving them into
one stark and simple
unity: the Cross.

He came unto His own —
loving, healing, teaching them, and
raising from the dead. But
His own received Him not —
hating Him, betraying Him, killing Him.

And all through that short and vibrant life,
He presented the face of God
to the face of evil.
'Crucify him', was their cry.
'Father, forgive them', His reply.

## SUFFERED

'Could you not watch with me one hour . . . ?'

Lord, what could it have meant to You
if the disciples had stayed awake and kept You company
in Your agony that night?
What did You hope for from their company?
Was it simply the knowledge of not being completely
alone?
Or was there something else,
something deeper, something
which to us would be
unguessable
but something which, in prayer and watching, they
could have supplied for You?

Whatever it was
it was denied You, and
you drank the cup of Your desolation
alone, while the disciples slept.

And what about today? What about now?
Do You ask me the same question?
Can I not watch with You one hour?
Are You asking me, Lord, to look at the world from the
vantage point of Gethsemane; inviting me
to explore the human element of that perfect faith
which kept You steady in Your great resolve?

Are You suggesting that I too look into the face of God
while the issues of life and death
take shape
and all that is against the truth assembles nearby
and angels come close to give their help?

Shall I not watch with You one hour?

Now?

Thank You Lord.
I have watched, and seen, and passed
through sorrow
into release : as if
through death to
resurrection.

Why is it, Lord, that I keep on denying myself by
denying You?

# UNDER PONTIUS PILATE

As I read of Jesus being brought into the Praetorium
I think of Paul and of all the occasions on which he
was hailed before the 'powers that be'.
And it occurs to me with fresh force, as if for the first
time –
(though it is not for the first time) –
that Paul went through a succession of such episodes,
that these were the arenas of his proclamation,
that his trials became his sermons;
that such an event as this became a recurrent part
of his missionary life.
So much was this the case, that to think of Paul creates
a frame of mind in which the thought of court room
and of judgement hall fits quite aptly and without
dissonance.

Not so with Jesus.
For Him there was one trial only, but one appearance
before a head of state,

only one stance before the judgement seat.

And how it jars with all the thoughts and images I have of the Lord –

to think of Jesus is to think of the preacher, the healer, the debater;

to think of Him is to think of the open air, the hedgerows and the flowers and the wayside, and the temple and the children, and cripples leaping with health and blind men seeing.

It is to think of dead men resurrected,

of storms stilled, of evil spirits cast out of tormented people,

of parties and feasts alight with gladness.

To think of Jesus is to think of life.

But now

my mind blunders into the judgement hall and sees

Jesus standing there

and it is all wrong.

The collision of mental images jars sickeningly in the mind.

I've always known it was vile. It's just that today I feel it.

It was all so stupid, too. For with His mind,

with His powers of discernment and judgement and with His spirit

it cannot be other than pathetic to see Him

arraigned before the logical outcome of stupidity,

avarice, evil, fear and ignorance.

And it is the abject pathos of it all which

wounds the mind and heart, and makes me want to run away from it.

For Jesus is not a pathetic figure. But the staggering thing is that He became one . . .

And now I remember words :
'No man takes my life from me, I lay it down of myself'.
And the pathos is transformed.
The tragedy and the sorrow are still there.
Indeed, the pathos remains there too, but it is
transformed.
For He did this willingly. He *became* a pathetic figure,
caught in a clumsy trap, snared by bungling and
incompetent people,
imprisoned by weaklings. No wonder He prayed 'If it be
possible, let this cup pass from me . . .'

For the doughty Paul, the judgement hall was a recurrent
pulpit. For Jesus it was the place of sublime self-giving . .
for all men, and for me.

# CRUCIFIED, DEAD AND BURIED

Three words which fall like hammer blows upon the
heart.
They speak of the reality of evil.
They speak of the reality of love.
They define the dimensions of my sin.
They reveal my value to God.

The scourge, the thorns, the nails, the spear :
the thirst, the taunts, the agony, the oblivion.
All this because of what I am, day by day.
All this the repercussion upon the divine, of my attitude
to life.
I, and all men.

Here at the Cross I meet myself.
Here I can come to myself.
Here – in His death – I can awake.

He died for me.
So that's what I'm worth to You, Lord. This much.
The value placed upon my head – upon the head of
each person – is measurable only in terms of
what Christ suffered
on the Cross.

These two shafts of light
intersect within my heart
like a cross.
My failure. My value.
Instead of remorse comes repentance. Instead of
despair comes hope.

## WHO DIED

It was
the One by whom the worlds were made
who suffered :
the maker of the minds which devised His death
who died.

No wonder
that skies were darkened and
earth trembled
when that heart
broke.

How can it be that some men's minds were
undisturbed?

Were the rocks more sensitive than they?

# A DELUSION DEALT WITH

I used to think that
the one insuperable barrier
between God and myself
was my sin.

Not that I believed God to be unforgiving by nature.
From childhood I had been told, and from
earliest memories
I had believed
that confession brings forgiveness.

The trouble was that no matter how carefully I confessed
new sins cropped up prolific beyond prevention.
So confession became a treadmill of the conscience,
a joyless necessity
in which one never advanced; a deadening drudgery
distracting me from life and love and weakening my
hold on God.

And then I saw the Cross again, and all was changed.
'He bore our sins in His body on the tree'.
'This is my body which is broken for you'.
'Your sins are forgiven'.

The dimensions of my forgiveness were revealed
by Christ upon the Cross.

He was God incarnate,
the One by whom the worlds were made, infinite
and eternal and
He
died that I might be forgiven.
The greatness of my forgiveness is measured by
His greatness.

Repentance is an attitude of the will, the heart,
and the mind, in which we share
our life
and therefore the knowledge of our sins
constantly with Him.
Forgiveness is the unending activity of God
contemporary with our every breath,
and like its giver it is
almighty and eternal.

# HE DESCENDED INTO HELL

Whatever else may be said of hell,
it is the end product of what happens to Man
when Man worships himself.

To worship myself is to depart from my true self.
It is to be alienated from what I am designed to be.
The consequences of that self estrangement
can be drawn out to the ultimate perspective of
horror.

Into this pit –
('My God, my God ! Why hast thou forsaken me?')
– Jesus descended.
I cannot think, or pray, or imagine myself into all that
this might mean.
I can only skirt the edge of this ocean of darkness.
But that He descended into hell;
that He plumbed the depths of this horror;
That He touched the bottom of the bottomless pit;
that He conquered and rose . . .
for all men, and for me,
this I believe.

# THE THIRD DAY

Not straight away. Not at once. Not
in the moment of time in which the veil was torn in two.
Not immediately in order to comfort and promptly to
assure
His stricken friends, His ravaged mother.
No.
He did not rise at once. But
on the third day. It was only
when the fact of death had arrived at successively deeper
levels into the disciples' minds; when information had
become knowledge;
when knowledge had become truth;
when all were quite sure He was dead :
it was only then that
He rose again.

Lord, when we wait for Your promises to come true,
give us patience, give us faith, give us hope,
give us obedience
to wait for
the
'third day'.

# HE ROSE AGAIN FROM THE DEAD

Lord, I've always felt that death is a nonsense.
But, if Jesus had not risen from the dead,
I could have no grounds for believing that it is.
But the fact is, Jesus rose.
This is not an article of faith : not really.
It is not a belief, requiring for its support
massive structures of faith and philosophy.
It is reported fact.
It is something observed, verified and reported
by the disciples.
To believe in the resurrection is to accept their report.
To disbelieve in the resurrection is to refuse it.
I cannot believe these witnesses to be either deluded
or deceitful.
Their character and actions, before, during and after
those three days
stamp them with every mark of veracity.
These are reliable men of many temperaments and
backgrounds,
with two things in common :
their honesty, and their statement that Jesus rose.

To disbelieve the resurrection would weaken any reason
I might have for believing any part of history.
To believe it changes my whole attitude to the universe.

# HE ASCENDED INTO HEAVEN

Lord, this idea of 'ascension' is oddly
welcome,
and that's surprising because
there was a time, not long ago, when
I couldn't really think about it, except in terms of
its physical impossibilities.

For how could a man,
hitherto held down by the forces of gravity,
rise through the skies
and go to heaven?

Now, however, while
not pretending to myself that I understand about
the relationship between matter and spirit, between
heaven and earth,
I find that the story of the ascension speaks to something
deep
inside me. And it comes to me each time I hear it,
as an ever more welcome guest.

Is this because the pattern-making mind of man
finds satisfaction in
a nicely rounded story with an ending both
happy and glorious?

Is it because of the confidence
thus declared by God
in the disciples, and the gratification
of knowing that, like them,
I am called to maturity and to the acts
of faith and of obedience
on which it rests?

Is it because this act of ascension
makes Christ contemporary? Transporting
Him from Galilee 2,000 years ago
into the present – eternally into the present,
ever to abide in the present.

Is it because His ascension puts us on the same footing
in our relationship with Him, as
Peter and James and John, and the others . . .?

Is it because
at the deepest level of the human heart
is the knowledge that heaven is where Christ
truly belongs . . .
the place of all power, the place of all glory,
there to be
unlimitedly
Himself?

## ON THE RIGHT HAND OF GOD

The lowly man in the place of supreme power.
The humble man in the throne of majesty.
The one who had nowhere to lay His head,
in the full possession of all things.
He who had sorrowed, triumphant.
He who is gentle, almighty.
He who hungers for righteousness, governing.
He who is merciful, interceding.
He whose heart is pure, counselling kings and seeing
all things.
He who is the peacemaker, reigning.
He who was persecuted for the cause of right,
revealing to all creation that almightiness is
indissolubly partner to humility.

# FROM THENCE

Heaven
is not just a place of
rest.
It is the seat of God's power.
It is the starting point of His purposes.
It is more like an engine room
than a paradisal beach.

But an engine room of such joy and concord
and fulfilled purposes
and realized desire,
that effort is
harmony
and all power is praise.

And out of this place of power
Christ will come again,
to be our judge.

Lord, I thank You that our knowledge of heaven
can grow upon earth.
For now I see it, not only as a place
to which will go all sinners who repent :
but also
as the place from which
the judge of all will come.

# TO JUDGE THE QUICK AND THE DEAD

I have a love-hate relationship with the thought of
judgement.
I can understand very well the 'hate' bit. What puzzles
me is where the 'love' comes from.
Like most people,
I hate the thought of someone outside myself passing
judgement on me – it's a hangover from childhood,
I suppose, inflated by pride, and enlarged by student
thoughts of examinations,
and service in the armed forces.
Everyone of us, I suppose,
including those who most conform to society's standards,
has a deeply rooted will to be independent of
external authority and judgement.

But there is that unexpected element of love there too.
I must explore that too, and try to trace its roots.
I think that it must come from the wish to know the
truth, the whole truth, and nothing but the truth about
myself.

I think I really do want to know even as I am known,
and that means that ultimately I want God's
definitive version of the truth about me to be shown
to me.
Even to state the thought is to quail at the prospect.
But the fear does not destroy the fascination.

## JUDGE JESUS

Lord, I know that the roots of my will are buried
deep
in selfish soil.
It is for that,
that men are judged.
But I have turned to You
despairing at my own complete inability
to live a genuinely generous
comprehensively holy life.
I am a sinner. And
there is a settled subconscious tenacity
about my selfishness.

But I have asked You, Creator Lord,
to recreate me,
through Christ and by the Spirit.

I do not know how I can live without that tap root
of selfishness driving down
deep within me.
But I have asked You to uproot it, Lord,
and plant it in the soil of Your love, Your grace,
Yourself.

And this, You assure us, is the prayer You never fail
to accept. You dwell within the sinner who repents.


Judgement?

I flee from it, and I flee to it.
I have good cause to do both.
But on those days when against all expectations I
desire it,

I think it must be
the movement of the Saviour within
towards the Lord in Heaven.


## THE HOLY GHOST

Help me, Lord, to understand the Holy Spirit.
I know this is a strange prayer.
It is strange because I know that
it is the Holy Spirit
who gives understanding.
So I will begin again : O Holy Spirit,
giver of understanding,
help me to understand You.

I have found that it is difficult to think about God
when I assume that He is
an object.
My thoughts only begin to come to life and work
when I *address* Him, when
in my prayer
the 'He' becomes a 'You', and when
thought becomes a conversation. Only then do I find
it possible
to think in a satisfying way about God.

It must surely be the same in my thinking about
Yourself, O Holy Spirit. For
You are God's spirit. You are God
reaching out to men.

It is because I think of 'spirit' as a 'thing',
an abstract 'thing', of course, but
a 'thing' just the same, that I have difficulty
in thinking about the Holy Spirit.

So I shall think of You as
God Himself
engaged
in a meeting with me
here and now,
and regard this as the way
to think of You.


## JESUS THE KEY

Jesus said,
'He who has seen me has seen the Father'.
and You, Holy Spirit, are the Father's life and power
reaching through all the universe.
Therefore,
Jesus shows us too, what You are like.

You are the Spirit who was active in Jesus.
You are the Spirit who required Him, through
temptation,
to find the methods to match His aim,
and even under greatest pressure, to make no pact
with evil.

You ar the Spirit by whom He conquered
all that made for evil, sin and death.

You are the Spirit by whom He chose,
and taught, and bore with His disciples.

You are the Spirit of the Lord
who was upon Him
anointing Him to preach the Good News to the poor,
who sent Him to proclaim liberty to the captives, and
recovery of sight to the blind, to set free the oppressed,

and to announce the year when God will save His
people.

You are the Spirit by whom, as heavy nails struck home,
He said: 'Father forgive'.

You are the Spirit by whom He rose and is alive for
evermore.

You are the Spirit given by Him, when He laid His
hands on the disciples, and said: 'Receive the Holy
Spirit'.

Holy Spirit, You link me directly with Jesus
and the Father
and all other disciples.
For You are one with the Father, one with the Son, and
dwell in
those who welcome You because of Christ.

O life, love, wisdom and power of the Father and the
Son,
You wish to enter me
at all times and
in this moment now.

Lord Spirit, come, dwell;
through me do the work of the Lord.

# THE HOLY TRINITY

'To what will you liken me?'

We ask You to speak, Lord, and among the things You
say is this!
'To what will you liken me?'

Once we hear this question, we may not set it aside.
O God, we speak of You as a Trinity:
Father, Son and Holy Spirit,
three persons in One God.

How far removed from life such language seems.
But it is the only way in which to speak about the facts.
For we cannot begin to think of Jesus
as He claims to have thought about Himself . . .
nor can we believe in Him as His disciples did . . .
without encountering
the absolute need for this strange mental apparatus.

When Jesus was baptized, we read that
the Father spoke, Jesus prayed, the Holy Spirit acted
simultaneously and in concert: each and all
simultaneously
living, working, reigning: each and all eternally
possessing the same personality, character and life.

But in speaking of You, Lord, as a Trinity, we are not
explaining You to ourselves.

I'm sure there can only be one God,
but on the other hand,
for all we know of 'godhead's' nature
He – the One God – may comprise *any* number of
'persons'.

He has revealed Himself in three.
He has declared the Three to be a Unity.
He has demonstrated that He is a Tri-Unity
– the Trinity.

O Lord, our doctrine of the Trinity is
a tribute to Your grace, and our ignorance;
the fulness of Your truth, and the limitations of our
mind.
You point out to us which way error lies.
You confine us to the facts.
In teaching us about Yourself, You tell us what belongs
together
in the tension of a mystery
we cannot understand.

To what shall I liken You, Lord?
You ask us the question, and we ask it, too, of You.
How lost we should be if You had not given us the
answer in Jesus.
Divine interrogator of man's conscience and imagination,
thank You for showing us the Christ; thank You
for the one who said :
'He who has seen me has seen the Father' . . .

For the same one who said : 'Receive the Holy Spirit',
for the self-same one who said : 'He who receives me
receives the One who sent me.'

Thank You for the clarity and simplicity of Your
answer : Jesus.
And thank You for the multi-dimensional,
omni-competent complexity
of Godhead
embodied
in Him.

O God the Father – origin; O God the Son – process,
pattern and brother;
O God the Holy Spirit – companion, life and guide;
O Blessed Trinity –
fulfilment and destination of all creation :
we believe.


## IMAGES OF GLORY

I thank You, Lord,
for all the images of Your glory
laid upon my mind
as a child.

They came from You, of course,
but they travelled many routes to reach me :
parents, neighbours, friends,
earth, sky, and sea,
pictures, music, books,
and
the Church.

And I thank You
in a specially intimate way
for that one particular church
which gathered together in my mind
the assorted images of Your excellence
and built them like a canopy around my head.

For the Sunday School which introduced me to those
life-long friends we find in the Bible,
clothing them in the mind with flesh and blood; and
for the church's little day school which,
simply by its existence,

taught me from the very first to think of all knowledge,
sacred and secular,
as one
and subject to Yourself.

For the Christian friends who
kept in kindly step as
adolescence brought the mind out of its childish world,
making it necessary to lay aside the
images of infancy
and live
as if the only context of my life
were dark and chilly streets, and the only
touchstone of all truth
a laboratory.

I thank You for the ones who provided me
with fresh data
for a fresh experiment
leading to a fresh encounter with Yourself,
enlarging, within their fellowship, my knowledge of
Your love
and helping me to find my way
back into the sort of church
I entered as a child, but now
with understanding and commitment.

Lord, I thank You for the Church.

# THE ONLY SOCIETY WHICH CAN

I thank You, Father, for the Church.
Oh, I know that
even among the faithful
this can be a most unfashionable,
even questionable,
cause for praise.
For the Church is the object, not only of its
enemy's attacks, but also the butt
of scorn and cynicism for many of those
who belong to it.

I thank You, Lord, that the Church,
at different times, and in different places,
and in different ways, has been and
is still
sufficiently itself
to deserve the attacks of those
who are Your enemies : enemies of
truth, enemies of goodness, enemies of beauty,
enemies of faith, hope, love; enemies of
Christ.

I thank You, too, that those who love it most,
resolutely refuse
to worship it, and avoiding this
idolatry,
learn to criticize creatively, as a lover and a friend.

But I am sorry that so many Christians
speak about the Church with so little love,
and so little humility.

Help us, Lord, to see that Christian criticism of the
Church
unwittingly is self-criticism. For how can I expect

the Church to be anything better than
my own response to God, writ large
and multiplied down the ages and
across the world.

I thank You for the Church, Lord,
because for all its faults it is the only
agency
through which
the Word of Life
reached me. No other society of people in the whole
range of time and space
could do for me
what the Church has done.

So I thank You for the Church, Lord,
the more so
as it ministers to me still.

# THE HOLY CATHOLIC CHURCH

The Church is holy, Lord –
so teach me the meaning of holiness;
for You are holy, and You are life.
And holiness, therefore, is
all to do with
life itself: life in all its dimensions,
life in all its beauty and power.

Where do we see holiness in action?,
In Gethsemane! On the Cross!
Beneath the Cross!

When Jesus prayed, and the disciples slept,
and His waking mind was all alone,
separated in the awful silence from
all conscious company,
Himself the one part of the seeing world,
truly
at one with its creator – there is holiness:
and then upon the Cross when, of all God's purposes,
He was the one strand which did not snap,
there in the moment of greatest stress,
('Father forgive them, for they know not what they do!')
was holiness.

And beneath the Cross holiness had new birth.
His mother Mary was there, seeing and
at some other but excruciating level, sharing in
the agony.
So too was John. Exposed
to all the dangers threatening from those who killed
the Christ,
they stood apart from the fearful,

out in the open, nakedly exposed
to the spectacle of God's love and anguish,
and
to the easy observation of a hostile world.

This was holiness.

Lord, teach us all to be holy.
Make Your Church holy.


## CATHOLIC

I thank You, Lord,
for Your power to hold
comprehensively within Your knowledge and Your love,
the whole motley multitude of
those who follow Jesus.

It is this power, Your power, which
makes the Church
Catholic.

I thank You that the Body of Your Son
is the home, the life, the freedom
of all who put their trust in Him :
people of all sorts and conditions,
all casts of mind, all colours of skin.

We have been, and still are
plagued and blessed
by our different traditions and denominations.
In our struggle to be united in our love for You, and
our service to the world; in our efforts to
show to each other and the world, the unity which

springs from Christ
we encounter problems
still several sizes too big
for the total brain power of the world-wide church
to solve.

Our unity, like our life itself, is hid
with God in Christ,
waiting to break out into history once more
(as did the early Church itself)
when Cross, and empty tomb, and Pentecost
are known, and seen and felt
again, by all.

Meanwhile,
we rejoice that
when we say : 'Jesus is Lord !'
You say : 'Amen !'
And all sorts of people from backgrounds
indelibly different
combine in Him to live anew.
People, with Christ in common,
holding the authentic faith of
incarnation, death and resurrection, by the gift of
the Spirit
throughout the world and down the ages :

It is our joy, our peace, our privilege and our hope
to be a member of this
Catholic Church.

# THE CHURCH

'Jesus is the Son of God. He loved me, and gave
Himself for me' . . .
and for every one of the world's teeming millions.

The whole machinery,
ecclesiastical,
theological,
academic, administrative, financial,
of the Church
exists
to make this one fact
known, understood and accepted
throughout the world,
throughout time.

Lord, help the whole Church to honour the word 'Lord'
when we speak to You.

# THE COMMUNION OF SAINTS

Lord, slowly I am learning that You are my life,
and I am learning that You are the life of all who
love You;
I am learning that we who love You share the same life,
and I am learning something of the sweetness and the
splendour of that sharing.
I am learning that when it is shared, our life in You
expands according to some inner principle
of spontaneous growth like fire.
And I remember that You are eternal. You do not die.
So that if You are my life, I shall not die.
And those who go before us with You as their life,
live in you still, as I do, as your family on earth does.

Lord as we worship You (You who are our life)
our love explodes across time and through eternity . . .
catching us together from both sides of death's division
and fusing our worship into one great act of
praise.

You are God –
not of the dead
but of the living.

# FOR OTHERS

This fellowship of believers brings its blessings, Lord,
assuring us, as it does, of the love and care
which others have for us. And so
I welcome its responsibilities – welcome them as
privileges – the charge we have from You, Lord,
to love and care for others.

So this prayer is not for myself, Lord,
it is for others.

I lay aside this syndrome of self-regard,
anxiety, hope, fear,
self-love,
and pray for others. And as I do so,
the weight which has been upon me
lifts.
I am free,
when I pray for others.

And as I glory in that new found freedom, Lord,
let it not detain me,
nor restrain me
now,
as I pray for others.

# THE FAMILY IN THE FELLOWSHIP

Lord, make us holy.
Lord, keep us safe and well.
In praying for my family, help me to pray this prayer
fully.
Lord, make us holy.
This must come first. It's hard
to ask for holiness before safety.
I want the safety and well-being of the family so much.
But everything I learn from the Bible
urges upon me the knowledge that I must learn
to ask first for
holiness.
What is holiness? There is the constant need to remind
myself of its true nature. It isn't
a confining, inhibiting perversion of puritanism.
It is complete givenness to the Father, and to His will
and purposes – it is the sort of givenness to God which
Jesus had on earth.
That sort of holiness is life abundant. It is the
fulfilment of true humanity. It is liberty and power and
peace.
It is, therefore, the greatest blessing I can ask for my
family.

Lord, keep us safe and well.
Why pretend that the safety and well-being of my
family is not of gigantic concern to me? To hide this
from anyone would be the sheerest hypocrisy. Besides,
it can bring me to my knees when other things cannot.

I think of the place of safety and well-being in the life
of the complete man – Jesus.

He was saved from harm again and again
'because His time was not yet come'.
Being in the centre of God's will was His safety till it became
His death and resurrection.


In praying for holiness
we are involving ourselves in God's will.
And God's will is our well-being with righteousness.
All Christ's healing ministry is a simultaneous declaration of two things:
His will that we be holy; His will that we be well.
'Your sins are forgiven. Get up and walk'.
That order is important. For Jesus made it clear that righteousness precedes well-being.


Lord, help me to pray for our holiness as fully as I can,
and do, pray for our well-being.
This will be the test of my faith.
It need not involve me in less prayer for well-being,
but it will involve me in more prayer for holiness.
In praying that they be holy I simply mean
that they will find all dimensions of reality in, and through
Christ; that He may evoke from them a glad and growing response;
that all the richness and warmth of humanity may be liberated within them as they – and I – leave all to follow Him.

# IN DEBT TO THE FELLOWSHIP

I thank You, Lord, for
all the great men of the Spirit
by whom You have spoken to me; through whom
You have called me.
How weak and wavering my response to You seems in
comparison with theirs. But I thank You for the
fellowship I have with them, and with all Your great
servants, in all ages, through the Community of Saints.

I know that the great Christians, by whom you have
blessed me, themselves
must fail.
Every Christian has feet of clay.
Each is at times aware of a weak and wavering heart,
but, despite their failings, I know that
through their ministry
has come to me the challenge of the ultimate and
absolute :
the Word of God, the command of Christ;
the incontestable presence of the eternal.
I thank You for the ministry of the Holy Spirit
through them.

And as I remember the weakness and the sin
which permeates my ministry to others,
I am thankful that this ministry is not mine, Lord, but
Yours. That same ministry exercised through that same
Spirit which reached me, and taught me marvellous
things.
This is the common factor in all Christian ministry —
whether it be that of the great men of my life
or my own faltering ministry now.
The common factor is
Your Holy Spirit, Lord.

For this I am glad, humble, relieved and
thankful.

Lord, grant me as Your servant one thing
and it shall be enough :
may the ministry in which I work be rooted
in Yourself.


## THE FORGIVENESS OF SINS

Jesus said, 'Father forgive them'.

He said it before the resurrection.
He said it when all His human experience, and all the
tortured fibres of mind and body,
heralded extinction.
He said it over the opening abyss, over the pit
of horrible darkness.
He said it before anyone had repented.
He said it while the mercy of oblivion was still hours
way.
He said it because it declared what He was in the
face of all evil.
So He overcame evil with good,
and triumphed over darkness.
Jesus said, 'Father forgive them', and
the Father
raised Him from the dead to live for evermore.

Thank You, Lord, for the mind of Your servants,
who in compiling the Creed, put 'the forgiveness of sins'
before
'the resurrection of the body'.
Forgiveness is the greater wonder; it is the mightier
marvel.

As God made all things out of nothing, so it is forgiveness
which makes a new relationship
out of the 'nothingness' of a broken relationship.
To forgive is
the most creative act
a human being can perform within a fallen world.
And it makes everything possible . . .


## REPENTANCE AND RENEWAL

Lord, forgive me . . .

Lord,
it's all these years
since my faith in You ceased to be subject
to my feelings
and instead, became a
resolute choice,
life-long by design and in intent.

It's all these years since I set out
deliberately
to be a disciple.

And I am learning that
every time I sin
I begin to die.
And every time I obey You, Lord,
new life begins.

Lord, let me live.

# RELIGION ISN'T GOD

It's humiliating to reflect that
I loved more when I knew less.
It's hard to admit that years of
thinking, reading, praying, preaching,
counselling and doing
all the hundred and one tasks of the Christian ministry,
do not add up to
greater love
for You, Lord.

I remember the early days of discipleship,
when my boats were burned and I was standing on a
new shore,
this side of my Jordan —
the days when
Christ was all in all.
The days when nimble-witted critics
and sardonic cynics could
shatter my defences
but couldn't touch my heart.

Now,
when the mind is secure,
it's the heart that's uncertain.
Now when I can, from long experience, shatter the
attack of the critic,
I've lost that purity of heart, that inner fire.

Touch me again, Lord.
Let me not prefer theology to You.
Let me not love religion : rather let me love You.
Let me not feel secure in my sound doctrine : rather let
me feel secure in Your service.

## AFTERMATH AND PROLOGUE

I thank You, Lord, for all that
follows repentance. For
newness.
Newness in my knowledge of You.
Newness in my love for You.
Newness in my knowledge of others.
And release of love for them as well.
For awakening. For liberation. And for growth.

For the sense of early morning in the heart.

# THE RESURRECTION OF THE BODY

Lord, we are in the realm of the unknown.
So many questions crowd the mind.
What are the facts we can grasp to begin with?

One fact is that this body lives, but one day will die.
That now it is, but one day will be no more.
Life is followed by death. And for the body,
death is followed by annihilation.

Another fact is that flesh and blood
survives. Men die. Flesh and blood
lives on.

Men inherit, inhabit, then shed it,
but always, and in every generation
they transmit it.

Against these first facts I put two questions.
One question is : do men acquire, use and shed the flesh
as if it were a chattel like a house or a car, something
other than
themselves?
Or is the connection
between soul and body more radical than that?

## CONNECTIONS

I know that the connections
between body, mind and spirit
are manifold and complex, at once
painfully and delightfully
real.

I know too
that the hold of the one upon the other is
complicated and tenacious,
separable
only by death.

This much I know. What else can I learn?
What does the Bible say about a man and his body?

## MAN AND HIS BODY

The Bible speaks of God
forming man from the dust of the earth and
breathing into him
the breath of life. It was from
this union of earth and spirit
that man took his being and became
a living soul.

The Bible also talks about the impact upon the
body
of the wrong man does,
so that in Adam
all die.

If we look at things this way
then obviously the body is more than a house for the
spirit.
There is an organic union between the two,
a union so profound
that when man revolts against the spirit which brought
him to birth,
revolts against his own foundation purpose,
revolts – that is to say – against God . . .
the repercussions of this revolt are felt
within the body.

# GOD IN HUMAN FLESH

God made another body. He made it
in the womb of Mary.
And it was Paul who said of
this new man, Jesus, that
He was the Second Adam. A Man whose body was
free
from the inroads of a sinful nature. Man
as man was meant to be, His body
the perfect instrument of a perfect spirit.

It was such a man —
a man in whom death had no claim —
who died upon the cross for us.

And His was the body
which sane men tell us
rose from the dead, and is alive for evermore.

# THE RESURRECTION OF HIS BODY

The question of whether I believe in the resurrection of
the body, turns
upon the question of faith in
Christ's resurrection. And I believe in that.
I believe in the resurrection of the body of Christ.
I cannot accept the view of those who say that
though His body died, His spirit lives for ever,
and that is what 'the resurrection' means.

I can't accept it because it does violence to the facts.
I can't accept it because it passes judgement on the
eye-witnesses.
I can't accept it because of what Jesus Himself said
about His own destiny.
I can't accept it because of the
incarnation.

For the one who became flesh was the Word by which
the worlds
were made. It was the creator
who made for Himself a body
and in it lived, and suffered and died.

And although it is possible to take the view
that the ultimate expression of His character and purpose
in His own world
is a dead body survived by a spirit believed to be alive —
to do so is to throw the mind into appalling conflict with
the rest of God's self-disclosure to mankind.

The historical evidence for the resurrection
is what persuades me to believe in it.
But having accepted it for this reason
I find this faith is buttressed

by the
internal logic
of Christianity itself.

\*\*\*\*\*\*\*\*

Jesus said to Thomas, 'Reach your finger here, see my hands. Reach your hand here and put it into my side. Be unbelieving no longer, but believe.' Thomas said, 'My Lord and my God!' Jesus said, 'Because you have seen me you have found faith. Happy are they who never saw me and yet have found faith.'*

*(John 20.27-29).

# THE SAME BUT DIFFERENT

What was His risen body like? It was a body
in character recognizably the same,
in performance observably different.

In some ways it was the same, for
He was visible, He was tangible. He could
see, hear, speak and eat. His hands could take bread
and break it.

But in some ways it was different. For now
His body exercised certain freedoms which
it had not exercised before. He appeared
to the disciples
as they hid behind locked doors, and He
disappeared from their sight. Finally
He ascended into Heaven.

The same, but different.
Lord, if it be possible,
help us to understand the sameness, and
help us to understand the
difference.
But above all help us to know You
the one unchanging Lord.

# AFTERWARDS

After the resurrection
the disciples remembered some words of Jesus
and saw them in a new light.
For one night He had taken bread and wine and said :
'This is my body – take and eat this. This is my blood –
everyone drink this.'

And the Spirit in the Church
taught them to see
themselves
as the Body of Christ,
living because He lives, sharing already in
His resurrection.

Our bodies are like
Adam's. But
they are inhabited by Christ
who gives to us His body and His blood.

And so if any man be in Christ he is a new creature.
God has begun a good work in him, and He will
perfect it.
It does not yet appear what we shall be like but we know
that when He shall appear we shall be like Him for
we shall see Him as He is.
We shall be the same, but different. Lord,
teach us to understand the sameness; teach us to
understand the difference.

# THE MIND OF THE MAKER

In the vastness of the universe
the planet earth is like
a grain of sand.
Within the scale of this comparison then,
our bodies are as tiny
as the universe is vast.

But we know our bodies to be the home of Spirit.
And we believe that it is Spirit –
God's Spirit –
who created matter.
And this Spirit – who created all things –
wishes to live in us.
So then what is within us is not within
stars and planets.
What is within God's sons is that which
made
stars and planeets.
Man did not make them. But he has been given the
Spirit
of Him who did.
Nevertheless, we shall die. The bodies in which the Spirit
dwells will disappear.

Can there be a resurrection of this body?
If God, who made all things, wills that there should be,
how can there not be?

The design of a building is known to its architect,
Though the building can be destroyed
the architect can rebuild, and his building can have its
resurrection body.

How much more is the design of our own self
known
to its maker and redeemer?
How much more wonderfully can He who made all
things recreate us, if He will –
not simply to be as we were
but to be as He intends.


## THE REAL TEST

'When I awake I shall be satisfied with thy likeness'*

When I awake?
Where, and from what?
When I awake in the great beyond, and from the
sleep of death?
*Then,* yes, then I shall be satisfied with Your likeness,
Lord.

Am I not satisfied now?
What satisfies me when I awake day by day, now, here?
Ambitions, desires, satisfactions, successes,
excitements . . . ?
Oh yes, all too often things like this.
And all the host of things with which I busy and
amuse myself day by day.

But what will these things count for when I awake at
the last
. . . that 'last' which is the great 'beginning'.
Will they count for anything then or will they
belong
to all the paraphernalia of self (which
like this body and the sin which does so easily beset me)
must be left behind?

If so, I must learn to leave them behind me now, this morning, now as I awake.

Let me instead be satisfied with Your likeness
today, tomorrow and the next day,
and the next.

*Psalm 17.15


## LIFE EVERLASTING

Everlasting life? Why,
it's inconceivable, Lord. Of course it is.
Even seventy years would be inconceivable without
the miracle of sleep,
and the many thousand little deaths
it brings to make life bearable.

But it's only inconceivable to us
as we are.
It's only inconceivable in terms of
time –
that 'linear concept' – that element
which we shall leave behind.

Life everlasting is life eternal, and –
of all things – God alone is eternal. Therefore eternal
life is – God's life.
God knows what eternity is
and if we live in Him He will teach us how to view it
and how to live it.
And if God is love, eternal life will give to love
its full expression.

Amen.

# ETERNITY

Eternity,
there's another thing.
I can't imagine, Lord.
But how well I remember thinking about it when
I was a child:
that night as the bedside candle flickered
and I thought of
for ever, and for ever, and for ever . . .
tasting the growing panic of a mind
which has ventured outside its confines and lost
the roots of its imagination.

Those roots are in the womb, no more than liberated
by birth
and surviving into that Eden paradise
of infant ecstasy
upon the mother's breast;
they are in the sculptured shadow of the father
who is present beyond, around and innately
within;
they are in the challenge, competition, collaboration
and delight
of brothers and sisters:
they are in the cosmic solidarity of the family.

And then people talked of heaven and of for ever,
and for ever, and for ever . . . and
the mind was torn up by its roots and rolled
like a young bush in a gale
around an empty landscape,
terrified :
till more by accident than design,
it returned to bed and candlelight and
'tonight' and 'tomorrow'.

What is eternity?
I still don't know, except that it is
a return to Eden,
with the Father present, escaped from shadow,
and with the splendour of creation
like the Mother's form and love;
and with the total complement of those brothers and
sisters of the blessed;
and with the cosmic solidarity of the universe
as it shall be.

Eternity is.
And it is a relationship.
Eternity is, and it is
a life
in which seed, root, flower and fruit
are one.

It is a dimension.
and it is for ever.

# THE MYSTERY OF TIME

How do we measure time, Lord?
By that quiet ticking on my desk,
that wrist watch with the broken strap
reminding me that I neglect the simple task of
mending it?
This little thing I never hear
when it's bound around my wrist, now loudly protesting
among my papers, tut-tutting away
at my conscience,
reminding me of time and of its passage,
and clicking its tiny tongue at my neglect.

Do we measure time by this little product of
men's nimble-fingered genius?

If not, how else?

By the slow arrival
like some reluctant tide
of grey hairs upon the head?
By the uprush growth of the children
whose baby length is still a part of present thought
even while they race their cycles, and start discussing
politics?

How shall I measure time?

By those long moments in the night
when the thought of death
takes shape,
becomes a thing to feel, and almost handle?
By the growing power to conceive of death in
physical terms,
as something enmeshed into the processes of this
familiar body?

As something which opens a door in the mind upon
the cry of Jesus:
'My God, my God, why hast thou forsaken me?'

How shall I measure time?

By the growing gift of understanding
of older people and of younger?
By the growing access to the mind and heart of Jesus?
By the growing knowledge that God enters our
mortality?
Emmanuel – God with us!

God with us in the reluctant tide of greying hairs
upon the head;
God with us in the body's slow decline;
God with us in the uprush growth of children;
God with us in that long momentary thought of death.

Keep clicking your tiny tongue, little watch.
We shall measure time by you, but
you are our creation, we are not yours.

And behind the hand that winds you up and gives you
life there is another timescale,
a timescale written deep into
our humanity.

How shall I measure time?
By the rise and fall of each
multi-cellular universe – each body?
By our response to Him who is eternal?
By an equation of the two?
So that in that rise and before that fall,

we meet and know and love, and bind ourselves unto
the One who died and rose again
and lives for ever :
the Eternal?

Oh yes, I think that's it.

# POSTSCRIPT — A NOTE ABOUT CREEDS

Creeds of one sort or another have always been an integral part of Christianity. The very first people who wished to join the community founded by Jesus expressed their faith in Him before being baptized. It could hardly have been otherwise. And the statement 'I believe' (in Latin : 'credo') has been an inescapable part of Christian commitment ever since.

The first creeds, then, were baptismal creeds, and they appear to have been both terse and pointed. 'Jesus is Lord' (1 Corinthians 12.3), and 'I believe that Jesus is the Son of God' (Acts 8.37) are thought to be typical statements of essential faith.

With the passage of time creeds became more comprehensive. But it was a relatively slow process. It may indeed be the case that something very like the Apostles' Creed was being used in Rome round about 150 AD. But there is no mention of it by this name until about 390 AD, and the earliest document known to quote it in its present form dates only from the 8th century.

Clearly then, we must not be misled by its name. It was neither composed nor recited by the Apostles. It bears their name because those among whom it evolved believed that it expressed what the Apostles themselves believed. In it we have a statement of Apostolic faith.

Creeds, however, were not only drawn up to serve the needs of Christian initiation. They were also formulated in order to define and so defend the essentials of the faith against the inroads of heresy. The work involved in this procedure was carried out at Councils of the Church, and a creed so formed, while often serving as a baptismal creed, is known as a Conciliar Creed.

Such, for example, is the one agreed upon at the Council of Nicaea in 325 AD, receiving some finishing touches at the Council of Constantinople in 381 AD. Known as the Nicene Creed, this is a familiar part of traditional Eucharistic liturgies.

Whereas the Apostles' Creed has been used chiefly in the Churches of the West, the Nicene Creed has been employed in Eastern and Western Churches alike. Members of the Anglican Communion will be well acquainted with both : the Nicene Creed in the service of Holy Communion; the Apostles' Creed in Morning and Evening Prayer.

## Godthoughts

Dick Williams, in this unusual book, attempts to get inside the mind of a young man feeling his way towards God, and taking his first steps as a believer. The poetic quality of much of the book makes it ideally suited to reading aloud.

## Meet Jesus

Geoff Treasure

A modern-day interpretation of St Mark's Gospel. It is written in an easy, conversational style, to introduce the person of Jesus and the meaning of the Gospel. (Published late 1973)

## He is everything to me

Ian Barclay

A devotional exposition of Psalm 23 all will find helpful, written in the readable style of one of today's popular preachers.

## The facts of the matter

Ian Barclay

A presentation of some basic Christian beliefs which reveals Ian Barclay's deep knowledge of his subject plus an awareness of our present world.